# Budget

What is a budget?
A budget is a spending plan determined by both income & expenses. Its formulated  to help estimate of how much money you'll make and spend over a certain period of time, such as a month or year.

# *Weekly* Budget / Expenses Log Sheet

Week of: _____     Beginning Balance: $_____

| Household Bills, Groceries, Car | | Miscellaneous Expenses | |
|---|---|---|---|
| | $ | | $ |
| | $ | | $ |
| | $ | | $ |
| | $ | | $ |
| | $ | | $ |
| | $ | | $ |
| | $ | | $ |
| | $ | | $ |
| | $ | | $ |
| | $ | | $ |
| | $ | | $ |
| | $ | | $ |
| | $ | | $ |

## {TOTAL}

| | |
|---|---|
| **BEGINNING BALANCE** | $ |
| **TOTAL WEEKLY EXPENSES** | $ |
| **ENDING BALANCE** | $ |

# *SAVINGS* Account Log Sheet

Beginning Balance_____ Month Of _____

| Date | Deposit Amount | Withdrawal Amount | Balance |
|---|---|---|---|
| | $ | $ | $ |
| | | | |
| | | | |
| | | | |
| | | | |
| | | | |
| | | | |
| | | | |
| | | | |
| | | | |
| | | | |
| | | | |
| | | | |

| Beginning Monthly Balance | Total Monthly Deposits | Total Monthly Withdrawal | Ending Monthly Balance |
|---|---|---|---|
| $ | $ | $ | $ |

**Note** Take the Beginning Balance, add Total Deposits, Minus Total Withdrawals* = Ending Balance**

# CHECKING Account Log Sheet

Beginning Balance_____ Month Of _____

| Date | Deposit Amount | Withdrawal Amount | Balance |
|---|---|---|---|
| | $ | $ | $ |
| | | | |
| | | | |
| | | | |
| | | | |
| | | | |
| | | | |
| | | | |
| | | | |
| | | | |
| | | | |
| | | | |
| | | | |

| Beginning Monthly Balance | Total Monthly Deposits | Total Monthly Withdrawal | Ending Monthly Balance |
|---|---|---|---|
| $ | $ | $ | $ |

**Note** Take the Beginning Balance, add Total Deposits, Minus Total Withdrawals* = Ending Balance**

# *Credit Card* Account Log Sheet

## Keep Track of Your Credit Card Balances

Credit Card Acct. # _____    Credit Card Acct. # _____

| Starting Balance | |
|---|---|
| Payment Amount | |
| Ending Balance | |

| Starting Balance | |
|---|---|
| Payment Amount | |
| Ending Balance | |

Credit Card Acct. # _____    Credit Card Acct.# _____

| Starting Balance | |
|---|---|
| Payment Amount | |
| Ending Balance | |

| Starting Balance | |
|---|---|
| Payment Amount | |
| Ending Balance | |

Credit Card Acct. # _____    Credit Card Acct.#_____

| Starting Balance | |
|---|---|
| Payment Amount | |
| Ending Balance | |

| Starting Balance | |
|---|---|
| Payment Amount | |
| Ending Balance | |

Credit Card Acct. #_____    Credit Card Acct. # _____

| Starting Balance | |
|---|---|
| Payment Amount | |
| Ending Balance | |

| Starting Balance | |
|---|---|
| Payment Amount | |
| Ending Balance | |

*Notes:*

_____

_____

# *Financial* Month in Review

## Savings Account Review
**Monthly Beginning Balance: $ _____**

**Month of: _____**

| Beginning Savings Balance For The Month | Total Savings Added This +Month | -Minus Total Withdrawals This Month | Ending Monthly Balance The Month |
|---|---|---|---|
| $ | $       +(plus) | -      (minus) | $ |

## Checking Account Review
**Monthly Beginning Balance $ _____**

**Month of: _____**

| Beginning Checking Balance For The Month | Total Added to Checking This + Month | Total Withdrawals This - Month | Ending Month Balance This Month |
|---|---|---|---|
| $ | $       + (plus) | $      - (minus) | $ |

*NOTES:* _____

_____

_____

_____

_____

_____

# *Weekly* Budget / Expenses Log Sheet

Week of: _____     Beginning Balance: $_____

| Household Bills, Groceries, Car | | Miscellaneous Expenses | |
|---|---|---|---|
| | $ | | $ |
| | $ | | $ |
| | $ | | $ |
| | $ | | $ |
| | $ | | $ |
| | $ | | $ |
| | $ | | $ |
| | $ | | $ |
| | $ | | $ |
| | $ | | $ |
| | $ | | $ |
| | $ | | $ |
| | $ | | $ |

## {TOTAL}

| | |
|---|---|
| BEGINNING BALANCE | $ |
| TOTAL WEEKLY EXPENSES | $ |
| ENDING BALANCE | $ |

# *SAVINGS* Account Log Sheet

Beginning Balance_____ Month Of _____

| Date | Deposit Amount | Withdrawal Amount | Balance |
|------|------|------|------|
| | $ | $ | $ |
| | | | |
| | | | |
| | | | |
| | | | |
| | | | |
| | | | |
| | | | |
| | | | |
| | | | |
| | | | |
| | | | |
| | | | |

| Beginning Monthly Balance | Total Monthly Deposits | Total Monthly Withdrawal | Ending Monthly Balance |
|------|------|------|------|
| $ | $ | $ | $ |

**\*Note\*\*** Take the Beginning Balance, add Total Deposits, Minus Total Withdrawals\* = Ending Balance\*\*

# CHECKING Account Log Sheet

Beginning Balance_____ Month Of _____

| Date | Deposit Amount | Withdrawal Amount | Balance |
|------|----------------|-------------------|---------|
| | $ | $ | $ |
| | | | |
| | | | |
| | | | |
| | | | |
| | | | |
| | | | |
| | | | |
| | | | |
| | | | |
| | | | |
| | | | |
| | | | |
| | | | |

| Beginning Monthly Balance | Total Monthly Deposits | Total Monthly Withdrawal | Ending Monthly Balance |
|---------------------------|------------------------|--------------------------|------------------------|
| $ | $ | $ | $ |

**Note** Take the Beginning Balance, add Total Deposits, Minus Total Withdrawals* = Ending Balance**

# *Credit Card* Account Log Sheet

## Keep Track of Your Credit Card Balances

Credit Card Acct. # _____

| | |
|---|---|
| **Starting Balance** | |
| **Payment Amount** | |
| **Ending Balance** | |

Credit Card Acct. # _____

| | |
|---|---|
| **Starting Balance** | |
| **Payment Amount** | |
| **Ending Balance** | |

Credit Card Acct. # _____

| | |
|---|---|
| **Starting Balance** | |
| **Payment Amount** | |
| **Ending Balance** | |

Credit Card Acct.# _____

| | |
|---|---|
| **Starting Balance** | |
| **Payment Amount** | |
| **Ending Balance** | |

Credit Card Acct. # _____

| | |
|---|---|
| **Starting Balance** | |
| **Payment Amount** | |
| **Ending Balance** | |

Credit Card Acct.# _____

| | |
|---|---|
| **Starting Balance** | |
| **Payment Amount** | |
| **Ending Balance** | |

Credit Card Acct. #_____

| | |
|---|---|
| **Starting Balance** | |
| **Payment Amount** | |
| **Ending Balance** | |

Credit Card Acct. # _____

| | |
|---|---|
| **Starting Balance** | |
| **Payment Amount** | |
| **Ending Balance** | |

*Notes:*

_____

_____

# *Financial* Month in Review

## Savings Account Review

**Monthly Beginning Balance: $ _____**

**Month of: _____**

| Beginning Savings Balance For The Month | Total Savings Added This +Month | -Minus Total Withdrawals This Month | Ending Monthly Balance The Month |
|---|---|---|---|
| $ | $      +(plus) | -      (minus) | $ |

## Checking Account Review

**Monthly Beginning Balance $ _____**

**Month of: _____**

| Beginning Checking Balance For The Month | Total Added to Checking This + Month | Total Withdrawals This - Month | Ending Month Balance This Month |
|---|---|---|---|
| $ | $      + (plus) | $      - (minus) | $ |

*NOTES:*_____

_____

_____

_____

_____

_____

# *Weekly* Budget /Expenses Log Sheet

Week of: _____  Beginning Balance: $_____

| Household Bills, Groceries, Car | | Miscellaneous Expenses | |
|---|---|---|---|
| | $ | | $ |
| | $ | | $ |
| | $ | | $ |
| | $ | | $ |
| | $ | | $ |
| | $ | | $ |
| | $ | | $ |
| | $ | | $ |
| | $ | | $ |
| | $ | | $ |
| | $ | | $ |
| | $ | | $ |
| | $ | | $ |

## {TOTAL}

| | |
|---|---|
| BEGINNING BALANCE | $ |
| TOTAL WEEKLY EXPENSES | $ |
| ENDING BALANCE | $ |

# *SAVINGS* Account Log Sheet

Beginning Balance_____ Month Of _____

| Date | Deposit Amount | Withdrawal Amount | Balance |
|---|---|---|---|
| | $ | $ | $ |
| | | | |
| | | | |
| | | | |
| | | | |
| | | | |
| | | | |
| | | | |
| | | | |
| | | | |
| | | | |
| | | | |
| | | | |

| Beginning Monthly Balance | Total Monthly Deposits | Total Monthly Withdrawal | Ending Monthly Balance |
|---|---|---|---|
| $ | $ | $ | $ |

**\*Note\*\*** Take the Beginning Balance, add Total Deposits, Minus Total Withdrawals\* = Ending Balance\*\*

# *CHECKING* Account Log Sheet

Beginning Balance_____ Month Of _____

| Date | Deposit Amount | Withdrawal Amount | Balance |
|------|----------------|-------------------|---------|
|  | $ | $ | $ |
|  |  |  |  |
|  |  |  |  |
|  |  |  |  |
|  |  |  |  |
|  |  |  |  |
|  |  |  |  |
|  |  |  |  |
|  |  |  |  |
|  |  |  |  |
|  |  |  |  |
|  |  |  |  |
|  |  |  |  |
|  |  |  |  |
|  |  |  |  |

| Beginning Monthly Balance | Total Monthly Deposits | Total Monthly Withdrawal | Ending Monthly Balance |
|---------------------------|------------------------|--------------------------|------------------------|
| $ | $ | $ | $ |

**\*\*Note\*\*** Take the Beginning Balance, add Total Deposits, Minus Total Withdrawals\* = Ending Balance\*\*

# *Credit Card* Account Log Sheet

## Keep Track of Your Credit Card Balances

Credit Card Acct. # _____

| | |
|---|---|
| Starting Balance | |
| Payment Amount | |
| Ending Balance | |

Credit Card Acct. # _____

| | |
|---|---|
| Starting Balance | |
| Payment Amount | |
| Ending Balance | |

Credit Card Acct. # _____

| | |
|---|---|
| Starting Balance | |
| Payment Amount | |
| Ending Balance | |

Credit Card Acct.# _____

| | |
|---|---|
| Starting Balance | |
| Payment Amount | |
| Ending Balance | |

Credit Card Acct. # _____

| | |
|---|---|
| Starting Balance | |
| Payment Amount | |
| Ending Balance | |

Credit Card Acct.# _____

| | |
|---|---|
| Starting Balance | |
| Payment Amount | |
| Ending Balance | |

Credit Card Acct. #_____

| | |
|---|---|
| Starting Balance | |
| Payment Amount | |
| Ending Balance | |

Credit Card Acct. # _____

| | |
|---|---|
| Starting Balance | |
| Payment Amount | |
| Ending Balance | |

*Notes:*

_____

_____

# *Financial* Month in Review

## Savings Account Review
**Monthly Beginning Balance: $ _____**
**Month of: _____**

| Beginning Savings Balance For The Month | Total Savings Added This +Month | -Minus Total Withdrawals This Month | Ending Monthly Balance The Month |
|---|---|---|---|
| $ | $      +(plus) | -      (minus) | $ |

## Checking Account Review
**Monthly Beginning Balance $ _____**
**Month of: _____**

| Beginning Checking Balance For The Month | Total Added to Checking This + Month | Total Withdrawals This - Month | Ending Month Balance This Month |
|---|---|---|---|
| $ | $      + (plus) | $      - (minus) | $ |

*NOTES:*_____

_____

_____

_____

_____

_____

# *Weekly* Budget / Expenses Log Sheet

Week of: _____     Beginning Balance: $_____

| Household Bills, Groceries, Car | | Miscellaneous Expenses | |
|---|---|---|---|
| | $ | | $ |
| | $ | | $ |
| | $ | | $ |
| | $ | | $ |
| | $ | | $ |
| | $ | | $ |
| | $ | | $ |
| | $ | | $ |
| | $ | | $ |
| | $ | | $ |
| | $ | | $ |
| | $ | | $ |
| | $ | | $ |

## {TOTAL}

| | |
|---|---|
| BEGINNING BALANCE | $ |
| TOTAL WEEKLY EXPENSES | $ |
| ENDING BALANCE | $ |

# *SAVINGS* Account Log Sheet

Beginning Balance_____ Month Of _____

| Date | Deposit Amount | Withdrawal Amount | Balance |
|------|---------------|-------------------|---------|
| | $ | $ | $ |
| | | | |
| | | | |
| | | | |
| | | | |
| | | | |
| | | | |
| | | | |
| | | | |
| | | | |
| | | | |
| | | | |
| | | | |

| Beginning Monthly Balance | Total Monthly Deposits | Total Monthly Withdrawal | Ending Monthly Balance |
|---------------------------|------------------------|--------------------------|------------------------|
| $ | $ | $ | $ |

**\*\*Note\*\*** Take the Beginning Balance, add Total Deposits, Minus Total Withdrawals\* **=** Ending Balance\*\*

# *CHECKING* Account Log Sheet

Beginning Balance_____    Month Of _____

| Date | Deposit Amount | Withdrawal Amount | Balance |
|------|------|------|------|
| | $ | $ | $ |
| | | | |
| | | | |
| | | | |
| | | | |
| | | | |
| | | | |
| | | | |
| | | | |
| | | | |
| | | | |
| | | | |
| | | | |
| | | | |

| Beginning Monthly Balance | Total Monthly Deposits | Total Monthly Withdrawal | Ending Monthly Balance |
|------|------|------|------|
| $ | $ | $ | $ |

**Note** Take the Beginning Balance, add Total Deposits, Minus Total Withdrawals* = Ending Balance**

# *Credit Card* Account Log Sheet

## Keep Track of Your Credit Card Balances

Credit Card Acct. # _____     Credit Card Acct. # _____

| | |
|---|---|
| Starting Balance | |
| Payment Amount | |
| Ending Balance | |

| | |
|---|---|
| Starting Balance | |
| Payment Amount | |
| Ending Balance | |

Credit Card Acct. # _____     Credit Card Acct.# _____

| | |
|---|---|
| Starting Balance | |
| Payment Amount | |
| Ending Balance | |

| | |
|---|---|
| Starting Balance | |
| Payment Amount | |
| Ending Balance | |

Credit Card Acct. # _____     Credit Card Acct.#_____

| | |
|---|---|
| Starting Balance | |
| Payment Amount | |
| Ending Balance | |

| | |
|---|---|
| Starting Balance | |
| Payment Amount | |
| Ending Balance | |

Credit Card Acct. #_____     Credit Card Acct. # _____

| | |
|---|---|
| Starting Balance | |
| Payment Amount | |
| Ending Balance | |

| | |
|---|---|
| Starting Balance | |
| Payment Amount | |
| Ending Balance | |

*Notes:*

_____

_____

# *Financial* Month in Review

## Savings Account Review
**Monthly Beginning Balance: $ _____**
**Month of: _____**

| Beginning Savings Balance For The Month | Total Savings Added This +Month | -Minus Total Withdrawals This Month | Ending Monthly Balance The Month |
|---|---|---|---|
| $ | $ +(plus) | - (minus) | $ |

## Checking Account Review
**Monthly Beginning Balance $ _____**
**Month of: _____**

| Beginning Checking Balance For The Month | Total Added to Checking This + Month | Total Withdrawals This - Month | Ending Month Balance This Month |
|---|---|---|---|
| $ | $ + (plus) | $ - (minus) | $ |

*NOTES:*_____

_____

_____

_____

_____

_____

_____

# *Weekly* Budget / Expenses Log Sheet

Week of: _____     Beginning Balance: $_____

| Household Bills, Groceries, Car | | Miscellaneous Expenses | |
|---|---|---|---|
| | $ | | $ |
| | $ | | $ |
| | $ | | $ |
| | $ | | $ |
| | $ | | $ |
| | $ | | $ |
| | $ | | $ |
| | $ | | $ |
| | $ | | $ |
| | $ | | $ |
| | $ | | $ |
| | $ | | $ |
| | $ | | $ |

## {TOTAL}

| | |
|---|---|
| **BEGINNING BALANCE** | $ |
| **TOTAL WEEKLY EXPENSES** | $ |
| **ENDING BALANCE** | $ |

# *SAVINGS* Account Log Sheet

Beginning Balance_____  Month Of _____

| Date | Deposit Amount | Withdrawal Amount | Balance |
|---|---|---|---|
| | $ | $ | $ |
| | | | |
| | | | |
| | | | |
| | | | |
| | | | |
| | | | |
| | | | |
| | | | |
| | | | |
| | | | |
| | | | |
| | | | |

| Beginning Monthly Balance | Total Monthly Deposits | Total Monthly Withdrawal | Ending Monthly Balance |
|---|---|---|---|
| $ | $ | $ | $ |

**Note** Take the Beginning Balance, add Total Deposits, Minus Total Withdrawals* = Ending Balance**

# CHECKING Account Log Sheet

Beginning Balance_____  Month Of _____

| Date | Deposit Amount | Withdrawal Amount | Balance |
|------|----------------|-------------------|---------|
| | $ | $ | $ |
| | | | |
| | | | |
| | | | |
| | | | |
| | | | |
| | | | |
| | | | |
| | | | |
| | | | |
| | | | |
| | | | |
| | | | |
| | | | |

| Beginning Monthly Balance | Total Monthly Deposits | Total Monthly Withdrawal | Ending Monthly Balance |
|---------------------------|------------------------|--------------------------|------------------------|
| $ | $ | $ | $ |

**Note** Take the Beginning Balance, add Total Deposits, Minus Total Withdrawals* = Ending Balance**

# *Credit Card* Account Log Sheet

## Keep Track of Your Credit Card Balances

Credit Card Acct. # _____

| Starting Balance | |
|---|---|
| Payment Amount | |
| Ending Balance | |

Credit Card Acct. # _____

| Starting Balance | |
|---|---|
| Payment Amount | |
| Ending Balance | |

Credit Card Acct. # _____

| Starting Balance | |
|---|---|
| Payment Amount | |
| Ending Balance | |

Credit Card Acct.# _____

| Starting Balance | |
|---|---|
| Payment Amount | |
| Ending Balance | |

Credit Card Acct. # _____

| Starting Balance | |
|---|---|
| Payment Amount | |
| Ending Balance | |

Credit Card Acct.#_____

| Starting Balance | |
|---|---|
| Payment Amount | |
| Ending Balance | |

Credit Card Acct. #_____

| Starting Balance | |
|---|---|
| Payment Amount | |
| Ending Balance | |

Credit Card Acct. # _____

| Starting Balance | |
|---|---|
| Payment Amount | |
| Ending Balance | |

*Notes:*

_____

_____

# *Financial* Month in Review

## Savings Account Review
**Monthly Beginning Balance: $ _____**
**Month of: _____**

| Beginning Savings Balance For The Month | Total Savings Added This +Month | -Minus Total Withdrawals This Month | Ending Monthly Balance The Month |
|---|---|---|---|
| $ | $      +(plus) | -      (minus) | $ |

## Checking Account Review
**Monthly Beginning Balance $ _____**
**Month of: _____**

| Beginning Checking Balance For The Month | Total Added to Checking This + Month | Total Withdrawals This - Month | Ending Month Balance This Month |
|---|---|---|---|
| $ | $      + (plus) | $      - (minus) | $ |

*NOTES:*_____

_____

_____

_____

_____

_____

# *Weekly* Budget / Expenses Log Sheet

Week of: _____     Beginning Balance: $_____

| Household Bills, Groceries, Car | | Miscellaneous Expenses | |
|---|---|---|---|
| | $ | | $ |
| | $ | | $ |
| | $ | | $ |
| | $ | | $ |
| | $ | | $ |
| | $ | | $ |
| | $ | | $ |
| | $ | | $ |
| | $ | | $ |
| | $ | | $ |
| | $ | | $ |
| | $ | | $ |
| | $ | | $ |

## {TOTAL}

| | |
|---|---|
| BEGINNING BALANCE | $ |
| TOTAL WEEKLY EXPENSES | $ |
| ENDING BALANCE | $ |

## *SAVINGS* Account Log Sheet

Beginning Balance_____ Month Of _____

| Date | Deposit Amount | Withdrawal Amount | Balance |
|---|---|---|---|
| | $ | $ | $ |
| | | | |
| | | | |
| | | | |
| | | | |
| | | | |
| | | | |
| | | | |
| | | | |
| | | | |
| | | | |
| | | | |
| | | | |

| Beginning Monthly Balance | Total Monthly Deposits | Total Monthly Withdrawal | Ending Monthly Balance |
|---|---|---|---|
| $ | $ | $ | $ |

**\*\*Note\*\*** Take the Beginning Balance, add Total Deposits, Minus Total Withdrawals\* = Ending Balance\*\*

# CHECKING Account Log Sheet

Beginning Balance_____ Month Of _____

| Date | Deposit Amount | Withdrawal Amount | Balance |
|------|----------------|-------------------|---------|
|  | $ | $ | $ |
|  |  |  |  |
|  |  |  |  |
|  |  |  |  |
|  |  |  |  |
|  |  |  |  |
|  |  |  |  |
|  |  |  |  |
|  |  |  |  |
|  |  |  |  |
|  |  |  |  |
|  |  |  |  |
|  |  |  |  |
|  |  |  |  |

| Beginning Monthly Balance | Total Monthly Deposits | Total Monthly Withdrawal | Ending Monthly Balance |
|---------------------------|------------------------|--------------------------|------------------------|
| $ | $ | $ | $ |

**Note** Take the Beginning Balance, add Total Deposits, Minus Total Withdrawals* = Ending Balance**

# *Credit Card* Account Log Sheet

## Keep Track of Your Credit Card Balances

Credit Card Acct. # _____

| | |
|---|---|
| **Starting Balance** | |
| **Payment Amount** | |
| **Ending Balance** | |

Credit Card Acct. # _____

| | |
|---|---|
| **Starting Balance** | |
| **Payment Amount** | |
| **Ending Balance** | |

Credit Card Acct. # _____

| | |
|---|---|
| **Starting Balance** | |
| **Payment Amount** | |
| **Ending Balance** | |

Credit Card Acct.# _____

| | |
|---|---|
| **Starting Balance** | |
| **Payment Amount** | |
| **Ending Balance** | |

Credit Card Acct. # _____

| | |
|---|---|
| **Starting Balance** | |
| **Payment Amount** | |
| **Ending Balance** | |

Credit Card Acct.# _____

| | |
|---|---|
| **Starting Balance** | |
| **Payment Amount** | |
| **Ending Balance** | |

Credit Card Acct. #_____

| | |
|---|---|
| **Starting Balance** | |
| **Payment Amount** | |
| **Ending Balance** | |

Credit Card Acct. # _____

| | |
|---|---|
| **Starting Balance** | |
| **Payment Amount** | |
| **Ending Balance** | |

*Notes*:

_____

_____

# *Financial* Month in Review

**Savings Account Review**
**Monthly Beginning Balance: $ _____**
**Month of: _____**

| Beginning Savings Balance For The Month | Total Savings Added This +Month | -Minus Total Withdrawals This Month | Ending Monthly Balance The Month |
|---|---|---|---|
| $ | $      +(plus) | -      (minus) | $ |

**Checking Account Review**
**Monthly Beginning Balance $ _____**
**Month of: _____**

| Beginning Checking Balance For The Month | Total Added to Checking This + Month | Total Withdrawals This - Month | Ending Month Balance This Month |
|---|---|---|---|
| $ | $      + (plus) | $      - (minus) | $ |

*NOTES:* _____

_____

_____

_____

_____

_____

_____

# *Weekly* Budget / Expenses Log Sheet

Week of: _____     Beginning Balance: $_____

| Household Bills, Groceries, Car | | Miscellaneous Expenses | |
|---|---|---|---|
| | $ | | $ |
| | $ | | $ |
| | $ | | $ |
| | $ | | $ |
| | $ | | $ |
| | $ | | $ |
| | $ | | $ |
| | $ | | $ |
| | $ | | $ |
| | $ | | $ |
| | $ | | $ |
| | $ | | $ |
| | $ | | $ |

## {TOTAL}

| | |
|---|---|
| BEGINNING BALANCE | $ |
| TOTAL WEEKLY EXPENSES | $ |
| ENDING BALANCE | $ |

# *SAVINGS* Account Log Sheet

Beginning Balance_____     Month Of _____

| Date | Deposit Amount | Withdrawal Amount | Balance |
|------|----------------|-------------------|---------|
|  | $ | $ | $ |
|  |  |  |  |
|  |  |  |  |
|  |  |  |  |
|  |  |  |  |
|  |  |  |  |
|  |  |  |  |
|  |  |  |  |
|  |  |  |  |
|  |  |  |  |
|  |  |  |  |
|  |  |  |  |
|  |  |  |  |
|  |  |  |  |

| Beginning Monthly Balance | Total Monthly Deposits | Total Monthly Withdrawal | Ending Monthly Balance |
|---------------------------|------------------------|--------------------------|------------------------|
| $ | $ | $ | $ |

**Note** Take the Beginning Balance, add Total Deposits, Minus Total Withdrawals* = Ending Balance**

# CHECKING Account Log Sheet

Beginning Balance_____      Month Of _____

| Date | Deposit Amount | Withdrawal Amount | Balance |
|------|----------------|-------------------|---------|
|  | $ | $ | $ |
|  |  |  |  |
|  |  |  |  |
|  |  |  |  |
|  |  |  |  |
|  |  |  |  |
|  |  |  |  |
|  |  |  |  |
|  |  |  |  |
|  |  |  |  |
|  |  |  |  |
|  |  |  |  |
|  |  |  |  |
|  |  |  |  |

| Beginning Monthly Balance | Total Monthly Deposits | Total Monthly Withdrawal | Ending Monthly Balance |
|---------------------------|------------------------|--------------------------|------------------------|
| $ | $ | $ | $ |

**Note** Take the Beginning Balance, add Total Deposits, Minus Total Withdrawals* = Ending Balance**

# *Credit Card* Account Log Sheet

## Keep Track of Your Credit Card Balances

Credit Card Acct. # _____

| Starting Balance | |
|---|---|
| Payment Amount | |
| Ending Balance | |

Credit Card Acct. # _____

| Starting Balance | |
|---|---|
| Payment Amount | |
| Ending Balance | |

Credit Card Acct. # _____

| Starting Balance | |
|---|---|
| Payment Amount | |
| Ending Balance | |

Credit Card Acct.# _____

| Starting Balance | |
|---|---|
| Payment Amount | |
| Ending Balance | |

Credit Card Acct. # _____

| Starting Balance | |
|---|---|
| Payment Amount | |
| Ending Balance | |

Credit Card Acct.# _____

| Starting Balance | |
|---|---|
| Payment Amount | |
| Ending Balance | |

Credit Card Acct. # _____

| Starting Balance | |
|---|---|
| Payment Amount | |
| Ending Balance | |

Credit Card Acct. # _____

| Starting Balance | |
|---|---|
| Payment Amount | |
| Ending Balance | |

*Notes:*

_____

_____

# *Financial* Month in Review

## Savings Account Review
**Monthly Beginning Balance: $ _____**
**Month of: _____**

| Beginning Savings Balance For The Month | Total Savings Added This +Month | -Minus Total Withdrawals This Month | Ending Monthly Balance The Month |
|---|---|---|---|
| $ | $      +(plus) | -      (minus) | $ |

## Checking Account Review
**Monthly Beginning Balance $ _____**
**Month of: _____**

| Beginning Checking Balance For The Month | Total Added to Checking This + Month | Total Withdrawals This - Month | Ending Month Balance This Month |
|---|---|---|---|
| $ | $      + (plus) | $      - (minus) | $ |

*NOTES:*_____

_____

_____

_____

_____

_____

# *Weekly* Budget / Expenses Log Sheet

Week of: _____   Beginning Balance: $_____

| Household Bills, Groceries, Car | | Miscellaneous Expenses | |
|---|---|---|---|
| | $ | | $ |
| | $ | | $ |
| | $ | | $ |
| | $ | | $ |
| | $ | | $ |
| | $ | | $ |
| | $ | | $ |
| | $ | | $ |
| | $ | | $ |
| | $ | | $ |
| | $ | | $ |
| | $ | | $ |
| | $ | | $ |

{TOTAL}

| | |
|---|---|
| **BEGINNING BALANCE** | $ |
| **TOTAL WEEKLY EXPENSES** | $ |
| **ENDING BALANCE** | $ |

# *SAVINGS* Account Log Sheet

Beginning Balance_____   Month Of _____

| Date | Deposit Amount | Withdrawal Amount | Balance |
|------|----------------|-------------------|---------|
|      | $              | $                 | $       |
|      |                |                   |         |
|      |                |                   |         |
|      |                |                   |         |
|      |                |                   |         |
|      |                |                   |         |
|      |                |                   |         |
|      |                |                   |         |
|      |                |                   |         |
|      |                |                   |         |
|      |                |                   |         |
|      |                |                   |         |
|      |                |                   |         |
|      |                |                   |         |

| Beginning Monthly Balance | Total Monthly Deposits | Total Monthly Withdrawal | Ending Monthly Balance |
|---------------------------|------------------------|--------------------------|------------------------|
| $                         | $                      | $                        | $                      |

**Note** Take the Beginning Balance, add Total Deposits, Minus Total Withdrawals* = Ending Balance**

# CHECKING Account Log Sheet

Beginning Balance_____ Month Of _____

| Date | Deposit Amount | Withdrawal Amount | Balance |
|---|---|---|---|
| | $ | $ | $ |
| | | | |
| | | | |
| | | | |
| | | | |
| | | | |
| | | | |
| | | | |
| | | | |
| | | | |
| | | | |
| | | | |
| | | | |
| | | | |
| | | | |

| Beginning Monthly Balance | Total Monthly Deposits | Total Monthly Withdrawal | Ending Monthly Balance |
|---|---|---|---|
| $ | $ | $ | $ |

**Note** Take the Beginning Balance, add Total Deposits, Minus Total Withdrawals* = Ending Balance**

# *Credit Card* Account Log Sheet

## Keep Track of Your Credit Card Balances

Credit Card Acct. # _____

| Starting Balance | |
|---|---|
| Payment Amount | |
| Ending Balance | |

Credit Card Acct. # _____

| Starting Balance | |
|---|---|
| Payment Amount | |
| Ending Balance | |

Credit Card Acct. # _____

| Starting Balance | |
|---|---|
| Payment Amount | |
| Ending Balance | |

Credit Card Acct.# _____

| Starting Balance | |
|---|---|
| Payment Amount | |
| Ending Balance | |

Credit Card Acct. # _____

| Starting Balance | |
|---|---|
| Payment Amount | |
| Ending Balance | |

Credit Card Acct.#_____

| Starting Balance | |
|---|---|
| Payment Amount | |
| Ending Balance | |

Credit Card Acct. #_____

| Starting Balance | |
|---|---|
| Payment Amount | |
| Ending Balance | |

Credit Card Acct. # _____

| Starting Balance | |
|---|---|
| Payment Amount | |
| Ending Balance | |

*Notes:*

_____

_____

# *Financial* Month in Review

## Savings Account Review
**Monthly Beginning Balance: $ _____**
**Month of: _____**

| Beginning Savings Balance For The Month | Total Savings Added This +Month | -Minus Total Withdrawals This Month | Ending Monthly Balance The Month |
|---|---|---|---|
| $ | $     +(plus) | -     (minus) | $ |

## Checking Account Review
**Monthly Beginning Balance $ _____**
**Month of: _____**

| Beginning Checking Balance For The Month | Total Added to Checking This + Month | Total Withdrawals This - Month | Ending Month Balance This Month |
|---|---|---|---|
| $ | $     + (plus) | $     - (minus) | $ |

*NOTES:*_____

_____

_____

_____

_____

_____

# *Weekly* Budget / Expenses Log Sheet

Week of: _____     Beginning Balance: $_____

| Household Bills, Groceries, Car | | Miscellaneous Expenses | |
|---|---|---|---|
| | $ | | $ |
| | $ | | $ |
| | $ | | $ |
| | $ | | $ |
| | $ | | $ |
| | $ | | $ |
| | $ | | $ |
| | $ | | $ |
| | $ | | $ |
| | $ | | $ |
| | $ | | $ |
| | $ | | $ |
| | $ | | $ |

## {TOTAL}

| | |
|---|---|
| **BEGINNING BALANCE** | $ |
| **TOTAL WEEKLY EXPENSES** | $ |
| **ENDING BALANCE** | $ |

# *SAVINGS* Account Log Sheet

Beginning Balance_____ Month Of _____

| Date | Deposit Amount | Withdrawal Amount | Balance |
|---|---|---|---|
| | $ | $ | $ |
| | | | |
| | | | |
| | | | |
| | | | |
| | | | |
| | | | |
| | | | |
| | | | |
| | | | |
| | | | |
| | | | |
| | | | |

| Beginning Monthly Balance | Total Monthly Deposits | Total Monthly Withdrawal | Ending Monthly Balance |
|---|---|---|---|
| $ | $ | $ | $ |

**Note** Take the Beginning Balance, add Total Deposits, Minus Total Withdrawals* = Ending Balance**

# CHECKING Account Log Sheet

Beginning Balance_____  Month Of _____

| Date | Deposit Amount | Withdrawal Amount | Balance |
|------|---------------|-------------------|---------|
|  | $ | $ | $ |
|  |  |  |  |
|  |  |  |  |
|  |  |  |  |
|  |  |  |  |
|  |  |  |  |
|  |  |  |  |
|  |  |  |  |
|  |  |  |  |
|  |  |  |  |
|  |  |  |  |
|  |  |  |  |
|  |  |  |  |
|  |  |  |  |

| Beginning Monthly Balance | Total Monthly Deposits | Total Monthly Withdrawal | Ending Monthly Balance |
|---------------------------|------------------------|--------------------------|------------------------|
| $ | $ | $ | $ |

**Note** Take the Beginning Balance, add Total Deposits, Minus Total Withdrawals* = Ending Balance**

# *Credit Card* Account Log Sheet

## Keep Track of Your Credit Card Balances

Credit Card Acct. # _____

| Starting Balance | |
|---|---|
| Payment Amount | |
| Ending Balance | |

Credit Card Acct. # _____

| Starting Balance | |
|---|---|
| Payment Amount | |
| Ending Balance | |

Credit Card Acct. # _____

| Starting Balance | |
|---|---|
| Payment Amount | |
| Ending Balance | |

Credit Card Acct.# _____

| Starting Balance | |
|---|---|
| Payment Amount | |
| Ending Balance | |

Credit Card Acct. # _____

| Starting Balance | |
|---|---|
| Payment Amount | |
| Ending Balance | |

Credit Card Acct.# _____

| Starting Balance | |
|---|---|
| Payment Amount | |
| Ending Balance | |

Credit Card Acct. #_____

| Starting Balance | |
|---|---|
| Payment Amount | |
| Ending Balance | |

Credit Card Acct. # _____

| Starting Balance | |
|---|---|
| Payment Amount | |
| Ending Balance | |

*Notes:*

_____

_____

# *Financial* Month in Review

## Savings Account Review
Monthly Beginning Balance: $ _____
Month of: _____

| Beginning Savings Balance For The Month | Total Savings Added This +Month | -Minus Total Withdrawals This Month | Ending Monthly Balance The Month |
|---|---|---|---|
| $ | $      +(plus) | -      (minus) | $ |

## Checking Account Review
Monthly Beginning Balance $ _____
Month of: _____

| Beginning Checking Balance For The Month | Total Added to Checking This + Month | Total Withdrawals This - Month | Ending Month Balance This Month |
|---|---|---|---|
| $ | $      + (plus) | $      - (minus) | $ |

NOTES:_____

_____

_____

_____

_____

_____

# *Weekly* Budget / Expenses Log Sheet

Week of: _____  Beginning Balance: $_____

| Household Bills, Groceries, Car | | Miscellaneous Expenses | |
|---|---|---|---|
| | $ | | $ |
| | $ | | $ |
| | $ | | $ |
| | $ | | $ |
| | $ | | $ |
| | $ | | $ |
| | $ | | $ |
| | $ | | $ |
| | $ | | $ |
| | $ | | $ |
| | $ | | $ |
| | $ | | $ |
| | $ | | $ |

## {TOTAL}

| | |
|---|---|
| BEGINNING BALANCE | $ |
| TOTAL WEEKLY EXPENSES | $ |
| ENDING BALANCE | $ |

## *SAVINGS* Account Log Sheet

Beginning Balance_____    Month Of _____

| Date | Deposit Amount | Withdrawal Amount | Balance |
|------|----------------|-------------------|---------|
| | $ | $ | $ |
| | | | |
| | | | |
| | | | |
| | | | |
| | | | |
| | | | |
| | | | |
| | | | |
| | | | |
| | | | |
| | | | |
| | | | |

| Beginning Monthly Balance | Total Monthly Deposits | Total Monthly Withdrawal | Ending Monthly Balance |
|---------------------------|------------------------|--------------------------|------------------------|
| $ | $ | $ | $ |

**Note** Take the Beginning Balance, add Total Deposits, Minus Total Withdrawals* = Ending Balance**

# CHECKING Account Log Sheet

Beginning Balance_____ Month Of _____

| Date | Deposit Amount | Withdrawal Amount | Balance |
|------|----------------|-------------------|---------|
|  | $ | $ | $ |
|  |  |  |  |
|  |  |  |  |
|  |  |  |  |
|  |  |  |  |
|  |  |  |  |
|  |  |  |  |
|  |  |  |  |
|  |  |  |  |
|  |  |  |  |
|  |  |  |  |
|  |  |  |  |
|  |  |  |  |
|  |  |  |  |

| Beginning Monthly Balance | Total Monthly Deposits | Total Monthly Withdrawal | Ending Monthly Balance |
|---------------------------|------------------------|--------------------------|------------------------|
| $ | $ | $ | $ |

**Note** Take the Beginning Balance, add Total Deposits, Minus Total Withdrawals* = Ending Balance**

# *Credit Card* Account Log Sheet

## Keep Track of Your Credit Card Balances

Credit Card Acct. # _____

| Starting Balance | |
|---|---|
| Payment Amount | |
| Ending Balance | |

Credit Card Acct. # _____

| Starting Balance | |
|---|---|
| Payment Amount | |
| Ending Balance | |

Credit Card Acct. # _____

| Starting Balance | |
|---|---|
| Payment Amount | |
| Ending Balance | |

Credit Card Acct.# _____

| Starting Balance | |
|---|---|
| Payment Amount | |
| Ending Balance | |

Credit Card Acct. # _____

| Starting Balance | |
|---|---|
| Payment Amount | |
| Ending Balance | |

Credit Card Acct.#_____

| Starting Balance | |
|---|---|
| Payment Amount | |
| Ending Balance | |

Credit Card Acct. #_____

| Starting Balance | |
|---|---|
| Payment Amount | |
| Ending Balance | |

Credit Card Acct. # _____

| Starting Balance | |
|---|---|
| Payment Amount | |
| Ending Balance | |

*Notes.*

_____

_____

# *Financial* Month in Review

## Savings Account Review
**Monthly Beginning Balance: $ _____**
**Month of: _____**

| Beginning Savings Balance For The Month | Total Savings Added This +Month | -Minus Total Withdrawals This Month | Ending Monthly Balance The Month |
|---|---|---|---|
| $ | $       +(plus) | -      (minus) | $ |

## Checking Account Review
**Monthly Beginning Balance $ _____**
**Month of: _____**

| Beginning Checking Balance For The Month | Total Added to Checking This + Month | Total Withdrawals This - Month | Ending Month Balance This Month |
|---|---|---|---|
| $ | $       + (plus) | $       - (minus) | $ |

*NOTES:*_____

_____

_____

_____

_____

_____

# *Weekly* Budget / Expenses Log Sheet

Week of: _____     Beginning Balance: $_____

| Household Bills, Groceries, Car | | Miscellaneous Expenses | |
|---|---|---|---|
| | $ | | $ |
| | $ | | $ |
| | $ | | $ |
| | $ | | $ |
| | $ | | $ |
| | $ | | $ |
| | $ | | $ |
| | $ | | $ |
| | $ | | $ |
| | $ | | $ |
| | $ | | $ |
| | $ | | $ |
| | $ | | $ |

## {TOTAL}

| | |
|---|---|
| **BEGINNING BALANCE** | $ |
| **TOTAL WEEKLY EXPENSES** | $ |
| **ENDING BALANCE** | $ |

# *SAVINGS* Account Log Sheet

Beginning Balance_____ Month Of _____

| Date | Deposit Amount | Withdrawal Amount | Balance |
|---|---|---|---|
| | $ | $ | $ |
| | | | |
| | | | |
| | | | |
| | | | |
| | | | |
| | | | |
| | | | |
| | | | |
| | | | |
| | | | |
| | | | |
| | | | |

| Beginning Monthly Balance | Total Monthly Deposits | Total Monthly Withdrawal | Ending Monthly Balance |
|---|---|---|---|
| $ | $ | $ | $ |

**Note** Take the Beginning Balance, add Total Deposits, Minus Total Withdrawals* = Ending Balance**

# CHECKING Account Log Sheet

Beginning Balance_____ Month Of _____

| Date | Deposit Amount | Withdrawal Amount | Balance |
|------|----------------|-------------------|---------|
| | $ | $ | $ |
| | | | |
| | | | |
| | | | |
| | | | |
| | | | |
| | | | |
| | | | |
| | | | |
| | | | |
| | | | |
| | | | |
| | | | |
| | | | |

| Beginning Monthly Balance | Total Monthly Deposits | Total Monthly Withdrawal | Ending Monthly Balance |
|---------------------------|------------------------|--------------------------|------------------------|
| $ | $ | $ | $ |

**Note** Take the Beginning Balance, add Total Deposits, Minus Total Withdrawals* = Ending Balance**

# *Credit Card* Account Log Sheet

## Keep Track of Your Credit Card Balances

Credit Card Acct. # _____

| | |
|---|---|
| Starting Balance | |
| Payment Amount | |
| Ending Balance | |

Credit Card Acct. # _____

| | |
|---|---|
| Starting Balance | |
| Payment Amount | |
| Ending Balance | |

Credit Card Acct. # _____

| | |
|---|---|
| Starting Balance | |
| Payment Amount | |
| Ending Balance | |

Credit Card Acct.# _____

| | |
|---|---|
| Starting Balance | |
| Payment Amount | |
| Ending Balance | |

Credit Card Acct. # _____

| | |
|---|---|
| Starting Balance | |
| Payment Amount | |
| Ending Balance | |

Credit Card Acct.#_____

| | |
|---|---|
| Starting Balance | |
| Payment Amount | |
| Ending Balance | |

Credit Card Acct. #_____

| | |
|---|---|
| Starting Balance | |
| Payment Amount | |
| Ending Balance | |

Credit Card Acct. # _____

| | |
|---|---|
| Starting Balance | |
| Payment Amount | |
| Ending Balance | |

*Notes:*

_____

_____

# *Financial* Month in Review

## Savings Account Review
**Monthly Beginning Balance: $ _____**
**Month of: _____**

| Beginning Savings Balance For The Month | Total Savings Added This +Month | -Minus Total Withdrawals This Month | Ending Monthly Balance The Month |
|---|---|---|---|
| $ | $      +(plus) | -      (minus) | $ |

## Checking Account Review
**Monthly Beginning Balance $ _____**
**Month of: _____**

| Beginning Checking Balance For The Month | Total Added to Checking This + Month | Total Withdrawals This - Month | Ending Month Balance This Month |
|---|---|---|---|
| $ | $      + (plus) | $      - (minus) | $ |

**NOTES:** _____

_____

_____

_____

_____

_____

# *Weekly* Budget / Expenses Log Sheet

Week of: _____    Beginning Balance: $_____

| Household Bills, Groceries, Car | | Miscellaneous Expenses | |
|---|---|---|---|
| | $ | | $ |
| | $ | | $ |
| | $ | | $ |
| | $ | | $ |
| | $ | | $ |
| | $ | | $ |
| | $ | | $ |
| | $ | | $ |
| | $ | | $ |
| | $ | | $ |
| | $ | | $ |
| | $ | | $ |
| | $ | | $ |

## {TOTAL}

| | |
|---|---|
| **BEGINNING BALANCE** | $ |
| **TOTAL WEEKLY EXPENSES** | $ |
| **ENDING BALANCE** | $ |

## *SAVINGS* Account Log Sheet

Beginning Balance_____ Month Of _____

| Date | Deposit Amount | Withdrawal Amount | Balance |
|---|---|---|---|
| | $ | $ | $ |
| | | | |
| | | | |
| | | | |
| | | | |
| | | | |
| | | | |
| | | | |
| | | | |
| | | | |
| | | | |
| | | | |
| | | | |

| Beginning Monthly Balance | Total Monthly Deposits | Total Monthly Withdrawal | Ending Monthly Balance |
|---|---|---|---|
| $ | $ | $ | $ |

**\*\*Note\*\*** Take the Beginning Balance, add Total Deposits, Minus Total Withdrawals\* = Ending Balance\*\*

# CHECKING Account Log Sheet

Beginning Balance_____  Month Of _____

| Date | Deposit Amount | Withdrawal Amount | Balance |
|------|----------------|-------------------|---------|
|      | $              | $                 | $       |
|      |                |                   |         |
|      |                |                   |         |
|      |                |                   |         |
|      |                |                   |         |
|      |                |                   |         |
|      |                |                   |         |
|      |                |                   |         |
|      |                |                   |         |
|      |                |                   |         |
|      |                |                   |         |
|      |                |                   |         |
|      |                |                   |         |
|      |                |                   |         |

| Beginning Monthly Balance | Total Monthly Deposits | Total Monthly Withdrawal | Ending Monthly Balance |
|---------------------------|------------------------|--------------------------|------------------------|
| $                         | $                      | $                        | $                      |

**Note** Take the Beginning Balance, add Total Deposits, Minus Total Withdrawals* = Ending Balance**

# *Credit Card* Account Log Sheet

## Keep Track of Your Credit Card Balances

Credit Card Acct. # _____

| | |
|---|---|
| **Starting Balance** | |
| **Payment Amount** | |
| **Ending Balance** | |

Credit Card Acct. # _____

| | |
|---|---|
| **Starting Balance** | |
| **Payment Amount** | |
| **Ending Balance** | |

Credit Card Acct. # _____

| | |
|---|---|
| **Starting Balance** | |
| **Payment Amount** | |
| **Ending Balance** | |

Credit Card Acct.# _____

| | |
|---|---|
| **Starting Balance** | |
| **Payment Amount** | |
| **Ending Balance** | |

Credit Card Acct. # _____

| | |
|---|---|
| **Starting Balance** | |
| **Payment Amount** | |
| **Ending Balance** | |

Credit Card Acct.# _____

| | |
|---|---|
| **Starting Balance** | |
| **Payment Amount** | |
| **Ending Balance** | |

Credit Card Acct. #_____

| | |
|---|---|
| **Starting Balance** | |
| **Payment Amount** | |
| **Ending Balance** | |

Credit Card Acct. # _____

| | |
|---|---|
| **Starting Balance** | |
| **Payment Amount** | |
| **Ending Balance** | |

*Notes:*

_____

_____

# *Financial* Month in Review

## Savings Account Review
**Monthly Beginning Balance: $ _____**
**Month of: _____**

| Beginning Savings Balance For The Month | Total Savings Added This +Month | -Minus Total Withdrawals This Month | Ending Monthly Balance The Month |
|---|---|---|---|
| $ | $     +(plus) | -    (minus) | $ |

## Checking Account Review
**Monthly Beginning Balance $ _____**
**Month of: _____**

| Beginning Checking Balance For The Month | Total Added to Checking This + Month | Total Withdrawals This - Month | Ending Month Balance This Month |
|---|---|---|---|
| $ | $     + (plus) | $    - (minus) | $ |

*NOTES:*_____

_____

_____

_____

_____

_____

# *Creditor-DEBT*-Pay Off Log Sheet

## (Keep track of your Creditor Debt) 12 Month Tracker

| Name of Creditor | |
|---|---|
| Account Number | |
| Credit Limit | $ |
| Starting Balance | $ |
| Interest Rate | % |
| Min. Payment | $ |
| Target Payoff Date | |

## {MONTHLY ENDING BALANCE}

| January | February | March | April |
|---|---|---|---|
| $ | $ | $ | $ |

| May | June | July | August |
|---|---|---|---|
| $ | $ | $ | $ |

| Sept. | Oct. | Nov. | Dec. |
|---|---|---|---|
| $ | $ | $ | $ |

Comments: _____

_____

_____

*This Log sheet is Designed to keep track of your Creditor Debt such as Credit Cards, Personal Loans, etc. This Log Sheet is Designed to keep track of One Creditor Debt over a 12 Month Period*

# *Creditor-DEBT*-Pay Off Log Sheet

## (Keep track of your Creditor Debt) 12 Month Tracker

| Name of Creditor | |
|---|---|
| Account Number | |
| Credit Limit | $ |
| Starting Balance | $ |
| Interest Rate | % |
| Min. Payment | $ |
| Target Payoff Date | |

## {MONTHLY ENDING BALANCE}

| January | February | March | April |
|---|---|---|---|
| $ | $ | $ | $ |

| May | June | July | August |
|---|---|---|---|
| $ | $ | $ | $ |

| Sept. | Oct. | Nov. | Dec. |
|---|---|---|---|
| $ | $ | $ | $ |

Comments: _____
_____
_____

*This Log sheet is Designed to keep track of your Creditor Debt such as Credit Cards, Personal Loans, etc. This Log Sheet is Designed to keep track of One Creditor Debt over a 12 Month Period*

# *Creditor-DEBT*-Pay Off Log Sheet

## (Keep track of your Creditor Debt) 12 Month Tracker

| Name of Creditor | |
|---|---|
| Account Number | |
| Credit Limit | $ |
| Starting Balance | $ |
| Interest Rate | % |
| Min. Payment | $ |
| Target Payoff Date | |

## {MONTHLY ENDING BALANCE}

| January | February | March | April |
|---|---|---|---|
| $ | $ | $ | $ |

| May | June | July | August |
|---|---|---|---|
| $ | $ | $ | $ |

| Sept. | Oct. | Nov. | Dec. |
|---|---|---|---|
| $ | $ | $ | $ |

Comments: _____

_____

*This Log sheet is Designed to keep track of your Creditor Debt such as Credit Cards, Personal Loans, etc. This Log Sheet is Designed to keep track of One Creditor Debt over a 12 Month Period*

# Creditor-DEBT-Pay Off Log Sheet

## (Keep track of your Creditor Debt) 12 Month Tracker

| | |
|---|---|
| **Name of Creditor** | |
| **Account Number** | |
| **Credit Limit** | $ |
| **Starting Balance** | $ |
| **Interest Rate** | % |
| **Min. Payment** | $ |
| **Target Payoff Date** | |

## {MONTHLY ENDING BALANCE}

| January | February | March | April |
|---|---|---|---|
| $ | $ | $ | $ |

| May | June | July | August |
|---|---|---|---|
| $ | $ | $ | $ |

| Sept. | Oct. | Nov. | Dec. |
|---|---|---|---|
| $ | $ | $ | $ |

Comments: _____

_____

_____

*This Log sheet is Designed to keep track of your Creditor Debt such as Credit Cards, Personal Loans, etc. This Log Sheet is Designed to keep track of One Creditor Debt over a 12 Month Period*

# *Creditor-DEBT*-Pay Off Log Sheet

## (Keep track of your Creditor Debt) 12 Month Tracker

| Name of Creditor |  |
|---|---|
| Account Number |  |
| Credit Limit | $ |
| Starting Balance | $ |
| Interest Rate | % |
| Min. Payment | $ |
| Target Payoff Date |  |

## {MONTHLY ENDING BALANCE}

| January | February | March | April |
|---|---|---|---|
| $ | $ | $ | $ |

| May | June | July | August |
|---|---|---|---|
| $ | $ | $ | $ |

| Sept. | Oct. | Nov. | Dec. |
|---|---|---|---|
| $ | $ | $ | $ |

Comments: _____

_____

*This Log sheet is Designed to keep track of your Creditor Debt such as Credit Cards, Personal Loans, etc.  This Log Sheet is Designed to keep track of One Creditor Debt over a 12 Month Period*

# *Creditor-DEBT*-Pay Off Log Sheet

## (Keep track of your Creditor Debt) 12 Month Tracker

| Name of Creditor |  |
|---|---|
| Account Number |  |
| Credit Limit | $ |
| Starting Balance | $ |
| Interest Rate | % |
| Min. Payment | $ |
| Target Payoff Date |  |

## {MONTHLY ENDING BALANCE}

| January | February | March | April |
|---|---|---|---|
| $ | $ | $ | $ |

| May | June | July | August |
|---|---|---|---|
| $ | $ | $ | $ |

| Sept. | Oct. | Nov. | Dec. |
|---|---|---|---|
| $ | $ | $ | $ |

Comments: _____
_____
_____

*This Log sheet is Designed to keep track of your Creditor Debt such as Credit Cards, Personal Loans, etc. This Log Sheet is Designed to keep track of One Creditor Debt over a 12 Month Period*

# *Creditor-DEBT*-Pay Off Log Sheet

## (Keep track of your Creditor Debt) 12 Month Tracker

| Name of Creditor | |
|---|---|
| Account Number | |
| Credit Limit | $ |
| Starting Balance | $ |
| Interest Rate | % |
| Min. Payment | $ |
| Target Payoff Date | |

## {MONTHLY ENDING BALANCE}

| January | February | March | April |
|---|---|---|---|
| $ | $ | $ | $ |

| May | June | July | August |
|---|---|---|---|
| $ | $ | $ | $ |

| Sept. | Oct. | Nov. | Dec. |
|---|---|---|---|
| $ | $ | $ | $ |

Comments: _____
_____

*This Log sheet is Designed to keep track of your Creditor Debt such as Credit Cards, Personal Loans, etc. This Log Sheet is Designed to keep track of One Creditor Debt over a 12 Month Period*

# *Creditor-DEBT*-Pay Off Log Sheet

## (Keep track of your Creditor Debt) 12 Month Tracker

| Name of Creditor | |
|---|---|
| Account Number | |
| Credit Limit | $ |
| Starting Balance | $ |
| Interest Rate | % |
| Min. Payment | $ |
| Target Payoff Date | |

## {MONTHLY ENDING BALANCE}

| January | February | March | April |
|---|---|---|---|
| $ | $ | $ | $ |

| May | June | July | August |
|---|---|---|---|
| $ | $ | $ | $ |

| Sept. | Oct. | Nov. | Dec. |
|---|---|---|---|
| $ | $ | $ | $ |

Comments: _____
_____
_____

*This Log sheet is Designed to keep track of your Creditor Debt such as Credit Cards, Personal Loans, etc. This Log Sheet is Designed to keep track of One Creditor Debt over a 12 Month Period*

# *Creditor-DEBT*-Pay Off Log Sheet

## (Keep track of your Creditor Debt) 12 Month Tracker

| Name of Creditor | |
|---|---|
| Account Number | |
| Credit Limit | $ |
| Starting Balance | $ |
| Interest Rate | % |
| Min. Payment | $ |
| Target Payoff Date | |

## {MONTHLY ENDING BALANCE}

| January | February | March | April |
|---|---|---|---|
| $ | $ | $ | $ |

| May | June | July | August |
|---|---|---|---|
| $ | $ | $ | $ |

| Sept. | Oct. | Nov. | Dec. |
|---|---|---|---|
| $ | $ | $ | $ |

Comments: _____

_____

_____

*This Log sheet is Designed to keep track of your Creditor Debt such as Credit Cards, Personal Loans, etc.  This Log Sheet is Designed to keep track of One Creditor Debt over a 12 Month Period*

# *Creditor-DEBT*-Pay Off Log Sheet

## (Keep track of your Creditor Debt) 12 Month Tracker

| Name of Creditor | |
|---|---|
| Account Number | |
| Credit Limit | $ |
| Starting Balance | $ |
| Interest Rate | % |
| Min. Payment | $ |
| Target Payoff Date | |

## {MONTHLY ENDING BALANCE}

| January | February | March | April |
|---|---|---|---|
| $ | $ | $ | $ |

| May | June | July | August |
|---|---|---|---|
| $ | $ | $ | $ |

| Sept. | Oct. | Nov. | Dec. |
|---|---|---|---|
| $ | $ | $ | $ |

Comments: _____

_____

*This Log sheet is Designed to keep track of your Creditor Debt such as Credit Cards, Personal Loans, etc. This Log Sheet is Designed to keep track of One Creditor Debt over a 12 Month Period*

# *Creditor-DEBT*-Pay Off Log Sheet

## (Keep track of your Creditor Debt) 12 Month Tracker

| Name of Creditor | |
|---|---|
| Account Number | |
| Credit Limit | $ |
| Starting Balance | $ |
| Interest Rate | % |
| Min. Payment | $ |
| Target Payoff Date | |

## {MONTHLY ENDING BALANCE}

| January | February | March | April |
|---|---|---|---|
| $ | $ | $ | $ |

| May | June | July | August |
|---|---|---|---|
| $ | $ | $ | $ |

| Sept. | Oct. | Nov. | Dec. |
|---|---|---|---|
| $ | $ | $ | $ |

Comments: _____

_____

_____

*This Log sheet is Designed to keep track of your Creditor Debt such as Credit Cards, Personal Loans, etc. This Log Sheet is Designed to keep track of One Creditor Debt over a 12 Month Period*

# *Creditor-DEBT*-Pay Off Log Sheet

## (Keep track of your Creditor Debt) 12 Month Tracker

| Name of Creditor | |
|---|---|
| Account Number | |
| Credit Limit | $ |
| Starting Balance | $ |
| Interest Rate | % |
| Min. Payment | $ |
| Target Payoff Date | |

## {MONTHLY ENDING BALANCE}

| January | February | March | April |
|---|---|---|---|
| $ | $ | $ | $ |

| May | June | July | August |
|---|---|---|---|
| $ | $ | $ | $ |

| Sept. | Oct. | Nov. | Dec. |
|---|---|---|---|
| $ | $ | $ | $ |

Comments: _____

_____

*This Log sheet is Designed to keep track of your Creditor Debt such as Credit Cards, Personal Loans, etc. This Log Sheet is Designed to keep track of One Creditor Debt over a 12 Month Period*

# *Creditor-DEBT*-Pay Off Log Sheet

## (Keep track of your Creditor Debt) 12 Month Tracker

| Name of Creditor | |
|---|---|
| Account Number | |
| Credit Limit | $ |
| Starting Balance | $ |
| Interest Rate | % |
| Min. Payment | $ |
| Target Payoff Date | |

## {MONTHLY ENDING BALANCE}

| January | February | March | April |
|---|---|---|---|
| $ | $ | $ | $ |

| May | June | July | August |
|---|---|---|---|
| $ | $ | $ | $ |

| Sept. | Oct. | Nov. | Dec. |
|---|---|---|---|
| $ | $ | $ | $ |

Comments: _____

_____

_____

*This Log sheet is Designed to keep track of your Creditor Debt such as Credit Cards, Personal Loans, etc. This Log Sheet is Designed to keep track of One Creditor Debt over a 12 Month Period*

# *Creditor-DEBT*-Pay Off Log Sheet

## (Keep track of your Creditor Debt) 12 Month Tracker

| Name of Creditor | |
|---|---|
| Account Number | |
| Credit Limit | $ |
| Starting Balance | $ |
| Interest Rate | % |
| Min. Payment | $ |
| Target Payoff Date | |

## {MONTHLY ENDING BALANCE}

| January | February | March | April |
|---|---|---|---|
| $ | $ | $ | $ |

| May | June | July | August |
|---|---|---|---|
| $ | $ | $ | $ |

| Sept. | Oct. | Nov. | Dec. |
|---|---|---|---|
| $ | $ | $ | $ |

Comments: _____
_____
_____

*This Log sheet is Designed to keep track of your Creditor Debt such as Credit Cards, Personal Loans, etc. This Log Sheet is Designed to keep track of One Creditor Debt over a 12 Month Period*

# *Creditor-DEBT*-Pay Off Log Sheet

## (Keep track of your Creditor Debt) 12 Month Tracker

| Name of Creditor | |
|---|---|
| Account Number | |
| Credit Limit | $ |
| Starting Balance | $ |
| Interest Rate | % |
| Min. Payment | $ |
| Target Payoff Date | |

## {MONTHLY ENDING BALANCE}

| January | February | March | April |
|---|---|---|---|
| $ | $ | $ | $ |

| May | June | July | August |
|---|---|---|---|
| $ | $ | $ | $ |

| Sept. | Oct. | Nov. | Dec. |
|---|---|---|---|
| $ | $ | $ | $ |

Comments: _____

_____

_____

*This Log sheet is Designed to keep track of your Creditor Debt such as Credit Cards, Personal Loans, etc. This Log Sheet is Designed to keep track of One Creditor Debt over a 12 Month Period*